It's the Little Things

IT'S THE LITTLE THINGS

The Pocket Pigs' Guide to
LIVING YOUR BEST LIFE

Photographs by **RICHARD AUSTIN**

WORKMAN PUBLISHING · NEW YORK

Library of Congress Cataloging-in-Publication Data is available.

ISBN 978-1-5235-0829-7

Cover photo by Richard Austin

Additional photo credit: Lucky-photo/Adobe Stock 31 (background)

Workman books are available at special discounts when purchased in bulk for premiums and sales promotions as well as for fund-raising or educational use. Special editions or book excerpts can also be created to specification. For details, contact the Special Sales Director at the address below or send an email to specialmarkets@workman.com.

Workman Publishing Co., Inc.
225 Varick Street
New York, NY 10014-4381
workman.com

Printed in China

First printing August 2019

10 9 8 7 6 5 4 3 2 1

Consider the Pig

As E. B. White taught us in *Charlotte's Web*, one should never underestimate the brilliance of a pig. And we humans have a lot to learn from them.

In an effort to be our best selves, we often reach so high that we forget to connect with the simple pleasures in life that truly make it worth living. But life on the farm is different. The slower pace, the routine, the fresh air, and the community of creatures big and small offer a perspective shift. As the Pocket Pigs of Pennywell Farm know, sometimes the littlest moments can harbor the greatest happiness.

These petite porcines may be unique in their stature, but they share the attributes of pigs of all sizes: They take care of one another, they're curious, they value a calm, tidy space (despite rumors to the contrary), and they relish the opportunity to learn something new. May we strive to meet every opportunity—big and small—with as much wonder, intelligence, and grace as the Pocket Pigs of Pennywell Farm.

You are allowed to be both a masterpiece and a work in progress, simultaneously.

—*Sophia Bush*

Live Life to the Fullest

In his book *The Whole Hog*, Johannesburg Zoo director and biologist Lyall Watson writes, "I know of no other animals [who] are more consistently curious, more willing to explore new experiences, more ready to meet the world with open-mouthed enthusiasm. Pigs, I have discovered, are incurable optimists and get a big kick out of just being." So the next time an opportunity comes your way, why not "go whole hog," as they say? Approaching life with joy, wonder, and an open heart is a great place to begin.

In the dew of little things the heart finds its morning and is refreshed.

—*Kahlil Gibran*

A champion is defined
not by their wins but
by how they can
recover when they fall.

—*Serena Williams*

Make Your House a Home

Pigs don't need much from their dwellings, just a spa (i.e., mud puddle), clean water, and a roof over their heads—shady in summer and toasty in winter. Like some humans, they also value coziness, and design their space to accommodate a communal lifestyle. That means a nest for pig piling and cuddling, but *not* a mess—contrary to what some popular idioms may suggest.

Find out who
you are and do
it on purpose.

—*Dolly Parton*

Dive Right In

They may not be able to fly, but guess what? Pigs can swim! Big Major Cay, aka Pig Beach, in the Bahamas, boasts a small colony of swimming feral pigs who are known to cavort with tourists frolicking in the waters. Legends abound about their origin— whether they were abandoned by a shipwreck or escaped from sailors who left them on the island, intending to eat them later. But they're not the only ones . . . landlubber pigs have been known to swim to safety during floods.

An adventure is
only an inconvenience
rightly considered.
—*Gilbert K. Chesterton*

Make Some Noise

Though real pigs may not be as articulate as Wilbur in *Charlotte's Web*, they do rely on verbal communication, using various types of grunts and squeals to tell other pigs how they feel. Some studies have shown that pigs can make up to twenty distinct sounds, which convey a wide range of information about their emotional state. And they are not afraid to make their voices heard—they can scream at volumes of up to 130 decibels. For comparison, a jet engine clocks in at 120 decibels, and a motorcycle maxes out at 88—no wonder a Harley-Davidson is called a hog!

Be strong, be fearless, be beautiful. And believe that anything is possible when you have the right people there to support you.

—*Misty Copeland*

Fortune Favors
the Bold

In Chinese culture, pigs are the last of twelve animals in the zodiac. A symbol of wealth, they are seen to represent good fortune, as well as honesty, abundance, and happiness. Those born in the year of the pig are believed to be intelligent, generous, curious, noble, and creative.

Joy does not simply happen to us. We have to choose joy and keep choosing it every day.

—Henri J. M. Nouwen

When you take a flower in your hand and really look at it, it's your world for the moment.

—Georgia O'Keeffe

Be a Good Listener

Say what? Just as pigs have very keen olfactory senses, they are also known for their sensitive hearing. Within a week of being born, pigs learn and will respond to their own names, and their moms communicate with them verbally as soon as they are born. Loud or high-pitched sounds will startle a pig, and long exposure to noise will stress them out, so it's important to speak softly and move carefully around pigs to keep them calm and comfortable.

Every day is perfect because there's no other day! . . . Every moment, every breath, every sound, every encounter is a gift. You bloody well better enjoy it.

—James Cromwell

Be a Hero

Pigs are intelligent, sensitive, and vocal creatures, making them perfect candidates for hero duty. And many have fulfilled the call—saving their human companions in emergency situations. A Pennsylvania-dwelling pig named LuLu once saved her owner Jo Ann, who was having a heart attack. When LuLu realized that something was wrong, she escaped through the doggy door and plopped down in the middle of the road, playing dead. A passing neighbor saw LuLu, noticed the scrapes on her belly from squeezing through the small door (which was far too narrow for her body), and went into the house to alert Jo Ann that her pig was injured. Instead, he found that Jo Ann herself was in distress, so he called an ambulance and saved her life.

Life is like
riding a bicycle.
To keep your
balance you must
keep moving.

—*Albert Einstein*

Don't Sweat It

Like many such sayings, the expression "sweat like a pig" is nonsensical—unless one sweats exclusively out of one's nose, it's impossible to sweat like a pig. That's because the only sweat glands on a pig's body reside in the snout.

In addition to their inability to regulate their temperature through sweating, pigs have tiny lungs, so they are physically limited to a lifestyle of moderate activity. Though pigs are sprinters and can quickly accelerate to up to 11 miles per hour, they cannot safely sustain that level of exertion. So think twice before you accuse pigs of being lazy, as they are actually practicing very necessary self-care.

If we don't have a sense of humor, we lack a sense of perspective.

—*Wayne Thiebaud*

Wear Sunscreen

With their dewy pink skin, it's no surprise that pigs are very sensitive to UV rays and are highly susceptible to sunburn. While shade and shelter are the protective measures of choice, if those are unavailable, pigs will opt for their favorite cure-all: mud. Cooling properties and sunblock? What more does a little pig need? The answer: insect repellent, and mud does that, too.

The joy of life
comes from our
encounters with
new experiences.

—Jon Krakauer

Treat Yourself

Just like dogs can learn to sit, stay, shake, or fetch, pigs can be trained, too—just imagine asking one to give hoof! But much like canines, they need incentives in order to learn. Luckily, they happen to be particularly treat-driven creatures. Training is easy once they figure out that the right behaviors mean a tasty reward. Among the safest and most preferred treats is popcorn (as long as it's unsalted, unbuttered, and air-popped).

One of the best ways to make yourself happy in the present is to recall happy times from the past.

—Gretchen Rubin

When you want to get good at something, how you spend your time practicing is far more important than the amount of time you spend.

—Joshua Foer

The biggest adventure you can take is to live the life of your dreams.

—Oprah Winfrey

Look After the Little Ones

Pigs are devoted moms. In the wild, they'll sometimes walk over six miles to find a secluded, peaceful place to give birth to piglets. They tend to stay separated from the herd for the first 24 hours after giving birth—remaining close to the nest with the babies and singing to them during feeding times.

Communication between mother and piglets is vital to the survival of the litter. Some species of fully grown female pigs can reach 500 pounds (compared to the 3- to 4-pound newborns), so a new momma will sing to communicate to her babies that she is about to lie down and they quickly learn to stay well out of her way. Then, using a series of short grunts, she lets them know that she is ready to feed them. She continues her lullaby at a rhythmic pace (in perfect sync with the suckling) and then shifts to a different grunt when feeding time is done.

Dare to Dream

When it's time for bed, pigs snuggle close to one another, sleeping snout to snout. They require a similar amount of sleep to humans—roughly eight hours per night—and even dream, though perhaps a bit less than people do. Pigs spend about 10 percent of their snooze time in REM sleep in comparison to humans, who average 25 percent.

HOLLYWOOD POCKET PIGS
PRODUCTION _____
DIRECTOR R. AUSTIN
CAMERA ONE
DATE   SCENE   TAKE

Remember: You must participate in the creative world you want to become part of.

—John Waters

Check Under the Hood

Like humans, pigs are extremely smart and thrive when mentally stimulated. They are believed to be the fourth most intelligent creature on earth. Pigs love a good treasure hunt, and like many animals, are motivated by food. Farmers or domestic pig owners sometimes hide treats in the dirt, hay, or sand for the pigs to discover. Or they'll pack smelly goodies into puzzle balls or dispensers, so the pigs really have to work to get the food inside. If a pig's environment does not offer enough to keep it busy, it becomes bored and its behavior will shift to frustration or even aggression.

Learning is a treasure that will follow its owner everywhere.

—*Chinese Proverb*

Don't Go Overboard

When tattooing became popular at sea, sailors would often adorn one foot with a tattoo of a pig. Legend had it that pigs would prevent shipwrecked sailors from drowning due to their deeply ingrained sense of direction—if something happened to the boat, the pigs would swim in the direction of the nearest shore. However, while aboard it was considered bad luck to mention land-dwelling creatures such as pigs and foxes. Woe might befall a seafarer who dared call them by name!

Rejoicing in ordinary things is not sentimental or trite. It actually takes guts.

—*Pema Chödrön*

Celebrate Happy Accidents

Before the dawn of modern banking institutions, hoarding gold at home in kitchenware was considered normal. In the Middle Ages, most kitchen items were crafted from an orange-colored clay called *pygg*. As the English alphabet evolved, pygg became *pigge* and then simply *pig*. So in nineteenth-century England, when potters were asked to make "pygg pots" for a customer, they delivered, in a lost-in-translation moment, a pig-shaped pot. And so was born the concept of a piggy bank: an iconic rite of passage and a way of teaching children about the value of savings.

If your dreams
do not scare you,
they are not big
enough.

—*Ellen Johnson Sirleaf*

Seek Comfort in a Tidy Space

Don't believe everything you hear—pigs are not dirty animals. In addition to being quite clean, they're also very focused on keeping their space neat (no shoes inside, please!) for their nest-mates. As long as they have sufficient room, they tend to keep their living spaces separate and are careful not to soil the area where they eat or sleep. And while they'll roll in the mud occasionally to keep cool or protect their skin, they very much prefer to bathe in water.

Acknowledging the good that you already have in your life is the foundation for all abundance.

–Eckhart Tolle

Be a Boss

While pigs tend to befriend their sty-mates, they still like to know who's in charge. When two pigs meet, one will immediately make a growling sound to assert her rank in the pecking order. The lower-ranking pig will step out of the way as asked. In larger groups, there is a head of the tribe—the matriarch—who can walk through the group, taking whatever bed she wants and feeding from whatever trough. Once that hierarchy has been established, it's rare that another pig will try to assert itself and disrupt the order.

Dogs look up to you, cats look down on you. Give me a pig! He looks you in the eye and treats you as an equal.

—*Winston Churchill*

The replenishing thing that comes with a nap—you end up with two mornings in a day.

—*Pete Hamill*

The most ordinary things could be made extraordinary, simply by doing them with the right people.

—Nicholas Sparks

Embrace the Journey

Domestic pigs are natural foragers and love to dig up root vegetables and hunt for truffles. While their big ol' snout is absolutely used for sniffing, it also works like a built-in shovel! The snout is an amazing creation—it is made of a round cartilaginous disc, which is connected to muscles that give it the strength and flexibility for rooting in the dirt for food. Pigs' impressive foraging skills include the ability to smell something buried twenty-five feet underground.

To love oneself is the beginning of a lifelong romance.

—Oscar Wilde

Snuggle Up

Pigs are affectionate and seek out not only the company of other pigs but physical contact with them, too. They are known to nuzzle snouts with each other when they are happy or excited, and when it's time to relax at night, they sleep cozied up in their nests. But their snuggles aren't limited to their fellow porcines—domesticated pigs love getting massages from their humans, and enjoy being physically close to creatures of all kinds.

To one in sympathy
with nature, each
season, in its turn,
seems the loveliest.

—*Mark Twain*

Savor the Moment

When it comes to food, pigs prefer to eat slowly and relish their meal, despite the common trope that suggests that pigs feast to excess, such as "eating like a pig" or "pigging out." They also have fantastic scent memories—they will remember and return to the spots where they've previously been fed or have discovered hidden food.

Life is always a rich
and steady time when
you are waiting for
something to happen
or to hatch.

—E. B. White

Be a
rainbow in
someone
else's cloud.

—*Maya Angelou*

It's Okay to Feel Things Deeply

Though appearances may suggest that they're tough customers with thick skin, pigs are quite sensitive emotionally and are known to cry real tears when they are sad or grieving. Confined spaces make them anxious, and domesticated pigs in particular get very upset when they are separated from their families—they become depressed and may refuse to eat.

How many times have you noticed that it's the quiet little moments in the midst of life that seem to give the rest extra-special meaning?

—Fred Rogers

I'm not afraid of storms, for I'm learning to sail my ship.

—Louisa May Alcott

Rely on Your Internal Compass

Much like dogs, pigs are known to have a good sense of direction and have found their way home over great distances. Their navigational talents may be linked to the fact that pigs have excellent sniffers. The sense of smell is closely linked to memory—likely more so than any other sense. They can recognize humans and up to thirty other pigs through smell alone.

Remember to look up at the stars and not down at your feet.

—Stephen Hawking

We can always begin again.

—Sharon Salzberg